The Truth about being a RainMaker

7 Principles for Sales Excellence

Rick Heyland

Copyright 2022 © Ci4life, LLC
All rights reserved. No part of this book may be reproduced or transmitted in any form or by any means, electronic or mechanical, including photocopying, recording or by any information storage and retrieval system, without written permission from the author, with exception for the inclusion of properly cited references and quotations.

ISBN: 979-8-82697-598-5

Cover Design: Andy Highland
Interior Design: Marianne Thompson

Dedicated to my colleagues at RLG International and our devoted clients who made these success stories, results, friendships, and learnings possible.

Book Recommendations

Rick has served as a trusted business advisor to me for the past 25 years and I highly recommend this book to anyone who is looking to improve their business sales growth. You will learn key principles and practices about building trusting relationships and client partnerships. Rick's lessons expressed in this book come from his own experience building client relationships, and take it from me, he knows how to do this. I consider Rick one of the few true personal friends I have made in my business career because he walks the talk. Rick, like his book, exudes authenticity and integrity, the stuff relationships are made from.

~Gary Lenett, Co-Founder and CEO of Pimlico Performance Apparel Ltd./DUER

If you're looking for continually becoming better in both your personal and professional career, Rick will break down how to become more trusted and sell! 5-Stars! Highly Recommend this book!

~John Rampton, Founder of Calendar.com and Due.com/Unicorn online business builder

In reading, *The Truth about being a RainMaker*, I found a lot of leadership traits explained that served me well in my 42-year career, even though I never was in sales. A common trait to be successful in either sales or leadership is trust. In working with Rick over a 5-year period, I found him to be a "Trusted Partner". This book spells out why that is important in sales and Rick and I also believe that it is important in life. Being a "Trusted Partner" allows the client to look at the consultant's fees as an investment and not just a cost.

Rick also spells out the importance of knowing your clients. In the 5 years that we worked together, Rick truly understood the demands on my time. When he sent me anything, he always took the time to summarize to make it easier on me. He would make a personal visit every 5 to 6 months to provide direct feedback on the performance of the organization that I led. He also would not waste my time with trivial items, but always focused on the key issues, both good and bad.

~Gary Yesavage, Former President of Chevron Manufacturing and Board Member of Big West Oil, LLC

I have known Rick for almost 20 years. This book is an easy read, yet comprehensively covers a subject that is complex and success is heavily correlated to effective, trusting human relationships.

The book brought back some very fond memories of my time in Alaska and the great engagement we achieved with the entire workforce through the effective design and execution of the Safety Performance Improvement program facilitated/coached by Rick and RLG. Lest we forget, the focus on safety also had a contingent effect of improving our operational efficiency as well.

I would highly recommend this book for anyone wanting to know how to improve their Sales, Client Management and Relationship Management.

~Gary Christman, Former VP of Energy Company

This book is a must-read classic for anyone who not only wants to become a better sales person, but a better person, period. Learning how to Make it Rain will empower you and create energy and drive to your everyday life. Read this book and learn from one of the best!

~Todd Sylvester, Mental Fitness Coach, Author, and Speaker. Top 5% Podcaster – Beliefcast (@toddinspires)

Having worked with Rick for years and seeing his success, we always used to ask, how does he do it? In this book, Rick has packaged and bottled it into something that's repeatable and useful both as fundamental and a structured process for great Business Development. So great, Rick. Thanks!

~John Shewfeldt, Vice President of RLG International

Rick's 7-step process for improving sales is as simple as it is powerful. With lots of success stories to illustrate his points, Rick's book will definitely get you fired up to 100x your sales!

~Brett Heyland, Owner/President of Candle Warmers Etc.

Rick has always been an outstanding partner. He seeks to understand, challenges you to be better, and always delivers - the recipe for Trust.

~Bill Ambrose, Expert Associate Partner, McKinsey & Company and Former Transocean Energy Executive

Table of Contents

Chapter 1 - Build a Systematic Process 1

Chapter 2 - Believe in your Cause .. 7

Chapter 3 - Know Your Avatar Customer 17

Chapter 4 - Become a Trusted Partner 23

Chapter 5 - Trust the Sales Process 41

Chapter 6 - The Business Development System 79

Chapter 7 - Continuous Improvement and Innovation 93

Chapter 8 - Be Your Best Everyday 101

Chapter 9 - Conclusion 117

About the Author 119

Acknowledgments 121

References 123

Chapter 1

Build a Systematic Process

If you're going to grow your business, you have to be good at sales.

Somehow being a salesperson has gotten negative connotations attached to it. But in fact, we are all salespeople. A doctor, dentist, teacher, scientist, and plumber are all salespeople. They have to effectively pitch and sell their ideas. If you are in any type of leadership role at home or work, you are in sales.

A RainMaker is defined as a person who attempts to cause rain to fall, either by rituals or by a scientific technique such as seeding clouds with crystals.

In the business context, a RainMaker is a person who generates income for a business or organization by brokering deals or attracting clients or funds.

Some people see Salespeople (or RainMakers) as pushy and always talking and trying to push their product no matter the relationship and cost. In this book, I will attempt to show you that Sales is a Noble cause and that being a RainMaker is the opposite of pushy, talking, and driving their own agenda. The real agenda for a Sustainable RainMaker has a much more worthy cause with skills and process that includes: customers needs first, Trust Building, and a true sense of why their product can benefit their Ideal customers. I will share this process in the 7 principles of Sales Excellence.

**Learn the Process
of being a True RainMaker**

Jerry Weisenfelder (current RLG International CEO) and I walked into an elevator in Alaska and on the way down from the 4th floor, we got a million-dollar order. "Rick, Jerry," he said, "Can you meet me tomorrow? We want to have some performance coaches on our team. I really like what I'm hearing from my sister organization." We laughed as we got out of the elevator and thought we were the luckiest people alive. A True RainMaker creates luck!

The backstory: We had just begun a large potential multi-year, multi-million-dollar program to help a company working the North Slope of Alaska to improve their safety results. The senior leader, Gary Christman, had taken a risk on us. Previously, we had only worked on productivity improvement programs. Gary had believed in our ability to implement the same coaching results in Safety performance. Four weeks into the pilot program, there was a serious accident on the work site. The client was nervous, an individual's future health and safety was at risk, and we were just at the beginning of the program for our team. We thought we might be fired. On Monday, Don Telfer (team leader) and I flew to the work site and spent the week learning and listening to what was going right and what went wrong. We came back down from the site on the following Monday and presented to Gary and his senior team our learnings and insights. They must have liked our approach and our insights because we ended up with one of the largest contracts in our company's history. We went on to replicate our program and our success throughout the whole world in our company and for our clients.

Why did I tell you this story? Because it illustrates the Sales system we built to grow our company 100x over 10 years in a very highly competitive management consulting industry.

I am ahead of myself. Let me tell you the whole story. I was the youngest hire in my company's history. Ten years later, I was the youngest senior manager in RLG International's history. I was promoted to run the Americas which was the largest region in our growing management consulting company. Then one year later, I was demoted to running one team in one state in the country. I was devastated, to say the least. I had a really good mentor, Rick Mazur, who put his arm around me and made me believe I could restart and be successful. He said, "You pride yourself on personal Continuous Improvement, don't you? It's part of your purpose, isn't it?"

"Yes," I answered.

"Then practice what you preach and figure out how to be successful and grow this company."

"Challenge accepted," I replied back.

Build and Trust a Process

"When you have a system, you kind of get in a routine of what's important. And then you spend a lot more time thinking of things that would make it better."
~Nick Saban

Nick Saban is one of the most successful coaches in NCAA football history. He has won a record 7 national titles. He has 109 active players in the NFL – another record. By most measures, he is the best of the best in his field. How does he do it? Great coaching? Great recruits? Yes, and he focuses on the process. He focuses the team on doing things the right way. He focuses his players on the process of being great every day and says the outcomes will come as a result.

It turns out that the same principle applies to building a great company and growing your sales.

On my second chance to lead this small part of our company, I made sure we learned and focused on building a process so we could build excellence in every day. I wanted to learn how to be a true RainMaker. It was at this point that I learned and developed this 7-point sales system that I am about to share with you. We went on to 100x our company's business over the next 10 years. I used to think it was about knowing your product, building relationships, and working hard, and you would be successful at selling and growing your business. From this experience and others, I learned there was much more to it than that.

Since retiring from full-time consulting in 2018, I have coached many salespeople and managers to implement this system with similar success. Let me describe to you in the following chapters how to make it Rain!

Pro Tip: Some of the chapters end with a practical Pro Tip that will help you apply the concepts taught in each chapter. The chapters also end with an Application Exercise section that has 2-4 questions to help you apply the principles to your business and your career. If you work through each one of these application exercises, you will finish this book with your own 7-step process to become the RainMaker in your industry!!

Chapter 2

Believe in Your Cause

There are so many products and services today. There are so many competitors. There are so many sharp salespeople.

There is also so much noise and clutter. Customers get bombarded every day with hundreds of emails and various forms of advertising. How is it possible to get through to your customer and convince them to buy?

The first step to do this is to Believe!

Nothing can stop somebody that believes in their cause.

If you believe in what you are selling, you will be more passionate, less discouraged, work harder, and be more motivated.

How do you define your cause?

Clarifying your purpose can help you develop your Cause.

There is so much research on the value of clear purpose to support high performance. Just

Google "value of purpose at work" or some variation of that and you will find a plethora of studies showing the correlation of high performance and clear purpose. Here are two examples:

Research shows[1] that companies with a strong purpose perform better on the stock market. A study of 20,000 employees showed that when leaders are clear about purpose, employees are about 100% more likely to stay in the organization.

Strong Purpose or a strong "Why" can help you perform better versus your peers. Employees enjoy their work and stay.

If you are selling, you need the benefit of clear purpose.

Purpose is defined as the fundamental reason the organization exists. Purpose is not your Vision or even your Values. Your purpose is not to make money. All organizations are meant to make money. That's not a bad thing. It's just not your purpose.

Remember Apple's original mission statement: "To have a computer on everybody's desk" (paraphrased). Google's is: "To organize the world's information". Those are both compelling statements that motivates every employee to work hard on behalf of the purpose.

Part of the original Apple cause was "Anti-IBM". Apple employees wore turtlenecks and IBM wore suit and ties. Apple wanted to get computers to the common person and IBM was for business. When Steve Jobs would stand up at their yearly company meetings, it was like a revolution, a cause for the people to join. Apple worked on Purpose!

Our purpose in consulting for 32 years was: "Implement Continuous Improvement with a bottom-line Result". We debated over the years, should we change that purpose/mission? But it continues to be the number one desire of corporate executives today. Therefore, we have not changed this purpose/mission statement in 35 years. We continue to innovate on how we deliver that value to our customer, but the promise to our customers remains the same.

Many companies had better processes, more articulate salespeople and consultants, but we delivered bottom-line results. We didn't get confused about what the senior client wanted. They wanted bottom-line improvement. For the clients that truly wanted that as their primary benefit, we won a high majority of the deals.

Aligned Personal Purpose Creates a Cause

The associates at McKinsey & Company have several pieces of great research on the value of purpose at work. Here is a quote from their May 2021 study:

"One of the things that we were surprised to find in the research is that about 70 percent of people say they define their purpose through work. And actually, millennials, even more so, are likely to see their work as their life calling."
~ Naina Dhingra

Millennial's make up a high percentage of the sales force today. We know from research that Millennials want to make a difference with their work, more so than any other generation. If you are a sales leader in an organization, make sure you have a clear purpose and cause. Make your work meaningful.

Again, from the McKinsey study:

"Nearly seven out of ten employees are reflecting on their purpose because of COVID-19. Those employees who say that they live their purpose at work are six and a half times more likely to report higher resilience."

We know the value of a more resilient workforce. They stay motivated, empowered, and are able to overcome setbacks.

As I discuss in more detail in my book, "Live Your Purpose", I developed a personal purpose/mission statement during a difficult time during my MBA Program. I was working very hard and was not doing well. I crafted my first draft of a purpose/mission statement during a troubling October weekend in the makeshift office of the unfinished basement in our home.

I didn't know at the time how important that purpose statement would be to my career and my life. That purpose statement said in part, "I desire to practice continuous improvement in my personal life and my career." When I found this small consulting company that practiced the very things I had in my purpose statement, I found energy, passion, and motivation. This purpose helped me overcome the discouraging setbacks along the path to 100x growth.

I highly encourage you and your organization to take the time to clarify and align around purpose. For more details on how to develop your purpose, please see this "Free Purpose Development" pdf on my website, www.ci4life.org.[2]

People always ask, how do you motivate your people? One of the ways employees stay motivated is if they have a clear sense of purpose and it aligns with what your organizational purpose is. Aligned purpose creates a huge and lasting sense of motivation. People and organizations that have purpose and believe in their product or service *work hard*! They don't mind hard work because it's fulfilling and helps drive meaning and contribution to life.

People also ask, how do you teach or encourage people to work hard? My answer is always the same: align around the purpose of your product/service and company, and people won't mind hard work. If people feel that their work is making a difference to their customers, they will work hard and be very motivated.

Find a Growth Cause

It's much easier to sell in a growth industry!

I have had over 1,000 coaching sessions with Millennials on career, sales, financial, and life management. I would be remiss if I didn't include this simple principle of following the growth. It will make it easier to 100x your sales if your cause has growth potential. Do you want to sell in the coal industry right now? That would be hard. But the renewables sectors are growing and will continue to grow. Over a 35-year sales career, I have had to pivot my Continuous Improvement brand to many sectors. Sales are always easier when the whole industry or sector is growing. When I give career advice to my Millennial friends who are building their career, I recommend that they find the intersection of 3 areas to find a successful career:

If you can find the intersection of these 3 questions, you will be unstoppable in your Sales career.

Are you passionate about it? Does it give you meaning & purpose?

Does it match your strengths?

Is it a growing sector?

John Rampton is a true online RainMaker. His purpose is to grow online Unicorn businesses. The online commerce business was $1.3 Trillion in 2014. In 2021, it was $4.9T and by 2025, it is projected to be $7.3T. John had a serious construction accident in his 20's that caused him to be immobile for some months. As he lay in the hospital and at home, he started online businesses. He hasn't stopped building those businesses since. One of his current businesses is Calender.com. He found a missing "value proposition" in the online calendar booking market, found a funding partner, and was off building another successful company. Driven by passion, enthusiasm, and the thought of making a difference in people's lives, John loves to work. He has told me several times that "work isn't work to me." He loves the challenge of growing something and adding value in the online marketplace. John exemplifies this concept of "believe in a cause." He is currently the marketing director (and part owner) of Gabb, a cell phone service for kids that offers protections and safety for child users. In 2021, he had $240M in online sales. He has built 4 unicorn online businesses over the last 10 years that have $18 Billion in online revenue directly attributed to his teams/companies. Find a Cause, Believe in your Cause, follow the growth, and work doesn't seem like work!

    Dave has been in Sales for most of his adult life. He has sold many types of products and services. He has done okay at times, but unmotivated and unhappy some of the time. He knew and practiced the type of Business Development system we suggest in Chapter 6. He tracked leading and lagging indicators and reviewed them weekly. He knew what to do but only had moderate success. He recently did an honest evaluation of his career and life and decided he wanted to move on to something that he really believed in. He wanted to make a difference and find purpose in what he was doing. He changed to a Medicare and Medicaid type company and is happier and more successful than he has ever been. "I finally feel that I am really making a difference in people's lives. It's the most rewarding job I have ever had."

Deon owned and ran a 1,700-person credit improvement business. Deon and his partner started the company from an idea and a piece of software. They sold that company to a private equity company after 20 years of growing the company and the industry. I will cite Deon's success story and some of the principles several times in this book because it follows closely with the 7-step process. His first principle for scaling a business is that you must believe you have a "life enhancing product or service." If you don't believe that, you will not be successful. "You and your team have to believe what you are selling matters and will make a huge difference in people's lives."

Do you really believe in what you are doing? Do you find real purpose in the value you are providing for the customer? If yes, continue on, learn the rest of this sales system, and become a true RainMaker in your industry. If the answer is no, find something that you can really believe in. You will never become a sustainable RainMaker and 100x leader if you don't believe.

You've got to Believe in your Cause and find purpose to be a Top RainMaker!

Application Exercises:
1. What is your purpose or cause?
2. What is your organization's purpose?
3. Can you concisely articulate the value your product/service offers the customer?
4. Are you able to act out your purpose in your current organization?

Chapter 3

Know your Avatar Customer

The meaning of Avatar is "embodiment" or manifestation of a person or idea.

The more you can articulate and understand your ideal client, the more success you will have in sales.

Know who your buying customer really is. Who is the decision maker? Whose vote counts the most? Know the title and position of that customer. What does that customer really want? What benefits do they most desire? Some consulting companies sold to HR professionals and they sold people benefits. We sold to the top of the house (president, VP, etc.) and sold bottom-line results. Our best customer was the Sr. VP of operations that wanted bottom-line improvement so they could go to their next board meeting and talk about tangible benefits. Take the time to dial in who the real buyers are for your product/service and what is the benefit they most desire. We did lose deals to other companies where the senior leader wanted better process or better training, but we rarely lost a deal when the senior decision maker was clear that the most important benefit was bottom-line change.

Having a clear picture of your ideal customer can save you time, money, and energy.

Too many organizations (or salespeople) are trying to be all things to all people. These types of organizations end up failing or not being as effective as they could. When you are focused on your ideal customer and their needs, you don't waste time making new products or services that they don't need or desire. Your whole organization is focused on pleasing one set of ideal customers. It creates a tremendous sense of focus and purpose. It allows your people to be the best at serving a specific customer rather than being average to all. Nobody wants to work for an organization that is making average services or products. Stay focused on your ideal customer and their specific needs.

Characteristics of your Avatar Customer

The most successful organizations can tell you the exact characteristics and demographics of their ideal customers. They can pinpoint the requirements to make a great win-win deal.

For example, in consulting, we knew our senior leaders needed a certain level of humility and openness to change. They had to be honest and "self-aware" enough to admit that they needed help and support. If their arrogance didn't allow them to admit they needed performance help, we were wasting our time.

You only have a certain amount of time and energy to close deals. It is the best use of your time and energy to focus on your Avatar customer with the right characteristics.

The competitive side of all of us wants to win all deals. I suggest that the best paradigm is to want to win all deals with your Avatar customer and his or her necessary characteristics. That doesn't mean that you should give up on people who initially don't seem to fit your Avatar customer characteristics. Some people show a different "first impression" until they trust. Later in this book, I share examples about Kevin and Larry who at "first impression" didn't show openness to change, but after we earned some trust, they opened up and showed tremendous openness to change and support.

As a general rule, I think we "hang-on" and keep trying with customers in our Customer Relationship Manager (CRM) for too long. Some people keep reporting at monthly meetings about the same 10 clients in the funnel because they don't want to give up on them. Many times, they are just wasting valuable energy.

Don't try and sell anybody and everybody. Have the wisdom to know when to move on. Clearly identify your strengths and determine the type of company and decision makers who value that strength. Here is one indicator that it's time to move on. Have you met 5+ times and they still are not showing the key characteristics of an ideal customer? For example, it's been 5 meetings and they still haven't admitted they need help. In this case, it is time to move on. This is a key step in becoming a RainMaker. You've got to be okay with losing some deals that don't match your strengths or ideals.

Successful online businesses do this step very well. All of the successful businesses online know exactly the customers they serve and their specific needs. Here are a few examples of either suppliers I have used or are clients:

1. Pat Flynn. The Smart Passive Income podcast and blog. Pat is the OG and go-to person on starting a podcast and doing passive income businesses. He was tremendously helpful as I started my own podcast: Continuous Improvement 4 Life (on Apple, Podbean, and other platforms). His ideal customer is people looking to start a podcast and to make passive income.
2. Dr. Ani Rostomyan. The Nutrigenomics Pharmacist. Her ideal customer is people

who are not being healed by traditional medicine. She offers a precision Health assessment and nutrition for your specific body.
3. Millennial Money.[3] It's my CI4life course helping Millennials (age 22-38) who want to build a high net-worth life, career, and finances.
4. Connor Dehlin. Millennial in Middle Podcast. A tremendously popular podcast for Millennials who are wanting to find the middle ground on hot political issues.

Pro Tip #2- Make a database with your top 25 ideal future customers. Include: organization, name, title, pain points, and characteristics. Use these categories as the columns on your spreadsheet or database. Update it regularly and review your last contact, learnings, and ideas for next steps.

Application Questions:
1. Who is your ideal customer?
2. What title and position do they hold?
3. What are the most important needs of your ideal customer?
4. What are the most important characteristics of your ideal customer?

Chapter 4

Becoming a Trusted Partner

This is such an important topic in the process of growing your business. My favorite author on this topic is Charles H. Green. He wrote a number of books including, "Trust-based Selling", "The Trusted Advisor", and "The Trusted Advisor Field Book". A summary of one of his main concepts is:

"The Goal of traditional selling is to convince the buyer to buy from you - the goal of trust-based selling is to help the buyer do what is right for him/her."
~Charles H. Green

This is such an important mindset shift. Before we dive into the details of the sales process and how to handle meetings, etc., I really want you to understand this overall strategy. You could be great in a meeting and do exactly what is tactically correct, but if you don't have the customers' needs in mind, you will not be successful in the long run. Do what is best for the customer – Always! Help the customer win and you will win. I know you have monthly sales quotas to hit. I know you feel the pressure of hitting these targets, but that is not the customers' issues.

Never Let the Customer See You Sweat

I used to tell this to my team all the time. Our budgets aren't the customer's concern. If our potential customers ever get a sense that we are working to meet our internal targets versus their needs, we have lost them as a long-term customer. You will never go wrong by putting the needs of the customer first. You may say to me, "What if I don't meet my quota by putting the customers' needs first?" I would answer, first of all, the two ideas are not mutually exclusive.

You can accomplish both. Secondly, that is why you build a large sales funnel. Not all deals will close within your internal timeline. So, you make sure you have done the work to build a funnel. It is an amazing feeling to have 10 customers in the closing process and you only need 5 of them to close to meet your internal targets.

You feel relaxed, and it's easy to put the customers' needs first because you have done the work to keep your pipeline full. I can name countless times when people lost large deals because the customer felt the pressure from the salesperson trying to meet their internal deadline. Put the client's agenda and timeline ahead of your own and you will build massive Trust.

Trusted Partner is More than Just a Relationship

I used to have leaders come to me all the time and say, "I have a great relationship with her, she will take my call anytime." I would reply, "If she has a need and she hasn't bought from you, then she doesn't trust you enough to buy."

Don't get me wrong. A relationship is great, but it is not the end. I don't mean to sound harsh, but we are not just talking about making best friends. It is comfortable to have people that like us and will go to lunch with us, but if you are truly a trusted partner, then they will also buy from you.

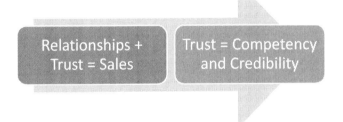

If you have my trust as a business partner, I believe you know your products and services and have the capability to do what you say you can do. This is so critical in sales. I may like you. I may go to lunch with you, but I won't buy from you unless I view you capable of helping me and doing what you are promising to do. How do you become more credible and competent? Go back to Step 1. Are you clear on your purpose? Your why? Are you clear on your value proposition to the world? Do you really believe it? If you can answer yes to these questions, you will "do the work" necessary to be competent and confident in your product. I don't want to burst your bubble, but if you don't really believe what you are selling will help change people's lives for the better, then quit and find a new service to sell that you can believe in. If you don't believe in it, clients can tell. You won't be viewed as trustworthy. Do your company and yourself a favor and find other products/services to sell that gives you passion. Then you will be a Trusted Partner. Then you will Make it Rain!

Principles and Steps to Become a Trusted Partner

For the initial sales meeting:

A. Preparation
B. Listen to Learn
C. Articulate with Confidence

Before your first sales meeting, do your homework and understand your potential customer's pain points as clearly as you possibly can.

Sometimes you can only come up with so much in your research session, so this is where listening comes into play. If you can, learn as much as you can in the first 15 minutes of the meeting. Yes, talk about football and the news, but when you get down to business, ask good open-ended questions to learn. For example, you may ask two simple questions.

Question 1. *I read that you guys have the best environmental track record in your industry. How did you accomplish that?* People love to tell you about what is going well, in particular, if they were a big part of it. This conversation can already start to build a relationship of trust. Don't jump right to the problem areas. Why? You put the client on the "back foot". You don't want to challenge your potential client before there is mutual respect and connection. Start with the strengths question or what is going well. Most of the time, they will love to tell you everything about it.

Question 2. *What are your areas for improvement? What goals for improvement do you have this year?* You want to make the question as safe and friendly as possible. My sales calls were always to senior people who have been successful in their careers and don't want to be challenged by anybody that doesn't respect them or understand their business.

Here is a good sample of open-ended questions so you can listen to understand their needs and pain points:

1. What keeps you awake at night?
2. Where do you see your company in 3-5 years?
3. What achievements are you most proud of?
4. What advice do you have for others who are trying to improve their results?
5. What areas are you most passionate about improving?

The Advice question is a real good one. Most people love to help and love to share their wisdom.

This doesn't mean you just listen for the whole meeting. Some leaders can use up the whole allotted time without giving you any time to tell your story. Remember to manage the agenda. After you learn, then you articulate how your product/service will help their specific pain points.

Sometimes first meetings don't go exactly as planned. I was in a boardroom once selling Larry, VP of Operations, for a large multi-national company. He was tough and to the point. He didn't want small talk or didn't want us to ask questions about their business. He wanted us to "dance first" to see if we knew our stuff. Luckily, we did significant homework and knew his industry and his company. We knew that maintenance turnaround times were very costly for him and they were in the 3rd quartile in their industry for cost and timeliness. We told him a similar experience we had in improving performance with this issue. He liked it. Ten minutes into our pitch, he started to tell us how some of their plants had similar problems and described the problems in some detail. We were taking copious notes and didn't interrupt him for 20 minutes. At the end of the meeting, he told his Number #2 person to give us a pilot at their New Jersey site. We started work at that site within a month. Our deals never go that fast. Usually, our multi-year, multi-million consulting engagements could take up to one year to sell. This was the exception. We went on to work at several of their plants and it was a large program for our company. I guarantee you if we hadn't done our homework and couldn't speak confidently and clearly about the issues and the solutions for maintenance turnaround, there wouldn't have been a second meeting.

Be Prepared with Insights that Build Trust

We prepared well for our meeting with Kevin. We found out he was a no-nonsense leader of a large multi-national company. He had taken his company out of bankruptcy and was proud of the recovery his company had achieved.

We were introduced to him by Gary Yesavage who was a past peer of his on an industry association. He didn't allow any time for chit chat or allow us to ask questions, but he had several questions for us. He described to us the problem he was having on a large capital project that was over cost and schedule. He described in detail the overages of materials and several other details and then asked us what we could do about it.

There was no time for generalities or platitudes. We needed specifics. Between my colleague and I, we outlined the process we would use in a phased approach to improve the project. He must have liked our insights and perspective because we landed an introduction to the project leaders that day. It turned out to be a long-term client as they had over 80 plants worldwide with many performance improvement opportunities.

You have to be prepared and speak with confidence about specifics in order to build credibility with seasoned senior executives.

With proper preparation comes confidence and courage!

Be Prepared, Clear, and Concise

Too many sales people just keep talking until something resonates with their potential client. To be a RainMaker, you have to learn to be clear and concise when it's time to talk. I first learned this lesson very early in my career when I went to my first sales meeting with my boss,

Keith Cross. We had a chance meeting in the hallway to visit with the potential buyer before our scheduled meeting. The buyer asked me how my work was going at his sister plant. I rambled on for a few minutes and then the conversation broke up. Keith took me around the corner and said, "Next time, be prepared with your elevator speech. Be clear and concise. For example, give him two things that were going well and one item that we are still working on." That conversation had a huge impact on me.

That was 35 years ago and I have never forgotten the valuable lesson of being prepared to capture a potential client's interest in 30 seconds or less. By the way, we did end up working with that client despite my poor start.

Be so prepared that you can say less!

Listen and Articulate Issues so Well that they are Nodding their Head

Roger Laing is the master articulator of clients needs. He asks powerful open-ended questions to have them articulate their needs and issues. He would then present back to them '3 things' that got their head nodding and responding, "That's exactly right." What a skill set to be able to ask great questions, listen carefully, and articulate the pain points. Talk about building trust! The client will often respond, "Yes, you really understand our needs."

Practice that skill set. Ask good questions, listen carefully, and articulate back the issues in such a way that it builds trust!

Go Slow to Go Fast if it Benefits the Client

I learned this lesson so many times in consulting work. It is better to set up the project/service well at the beginning with clear expectations, plans, and agreements than rush to failure. This principle also applies to sales.

I had been in the business development process with a large client in Houston for several months when we got a chance to show them what we could do. They were a large multi-national client with offices all over the world. They were also underperforming and struggling with large downtime issues at their facilities. The size of the prize was huge. It was apparent they were a perfect match for our Avatar client. They had a large business need and they knew they needed help. The senior leader, Bill Ambrose, had a vision of what he wanted done, but knew they didn't have a lot of time to turn things around. They were starting to lose work around the world because of poor performance. I was able to sell them a four-week assessment. I called up my colleague, Chris Payne, and he was in Houston the next day to begin the work. I saw the huge benefit we could provide for them, their clients, and our own bottom-line. The stakes were high.

I still remember where I was sitting on my back deck when Chris and his team reviewed with me their preliminary findings and recommendations before we presented to the client. They recommended we start with two project managers to fix the Houston process before we went out to the world to help their maintenance work. Chris said, "We need to go slow to go fast. We need to rectify their internal processes first before we can go out and fix their work around the world." He was recommending a $500,000 deal and I was anticipating a $5M deal. I was upset. I can only remember getting mad at my team three times (there may have been more but that's all I can remember!). Chris remained patient with me and resolute on their recommendation. "This is the best thing for this client. We can't go out to the world and try and improve broken processes." After I cooled down, I knew he was right.

With Bill Ambrose's strong leadership and support, we made a one-billion-dollar turnaround for that client over the next three years. Bill and Chris partnered so well together. The trust was so high between us and him that we formed a long-term relationship that has lasted for many years. It turned out to be great for our company as well. Chris got a promotion to lead a new business unit in my group and the work turned out to be double the amount I had originally projected. Chris still reminds me of that conversation. I am so glad they stuck to their guns and put what was best for the client first. It built incredible trust with the client!!!

Consistency and Long-term Thinking

Do you want to move from being a vendor to a trusted partner? Then apply these two simple principles of Consistency and Long-term Thinking. Not all contacts will move to done deal on the first cycle. You must find "value add" ways to keep in contact with your Avatar potential customer. If you don't, you are out of sight and out of mind. You have to be creative and "value add" so you don't come off as a pest. You must find valuable ways to keep in contact.

Here are some of my favorites.

1. Send them an article of interest to them. They may not have time to read the article so summarize a key point or underline it. Respect their time; they are busy. Make it easy to digest the key points and to put you on "top of mind".
2. Invite them to a networking lunch with other key executives. It is of huge value for them to stay connected with people at the same levels in other companies.
3. Invite them to lunch to connect and share your latest insights and learnings. You can also act as a coach and help them think through a problem.

4. Email them a sports update about their favorite team.
5. Share with them a success story about your company that may be of interest to them. A humble brag.
6. Contact them on social media on their birthday.
7. Invite them to your annual meeting.
8. Search publications for success stories about their companies and send congratulation notes to them.
9. Introduce them to somebody that can help their career or company.
10. Have a Zoom/Teams call with each leader to update them on your progress and to hear the latest about the companies' needs. In our Post-Covid world, customers are very open to quick check-ins that don't take away from their busy agendas.

We stayed connected with Bill Ambrose after the previous $1B turnaround story. He was a great leader and was aligned with our methods. He moved on to a corporate role and wasn't a 'check-signer' now, but we stayed connected with him. He made himself available for lunches when we came to town. He would come to our network lunches. He attended our "Best of the Best" annual meetings. When he was promoted again two years later, we secured the largest single deal in our company's history to help improve performance in his operations.

With Bill and Bill Nash's (RLG leader) leadership, we made a second major turnaround in performance for that company.

The Value of Repeat Customers

Taylor Landis writes an interesting business strategy and sales blog. She did a great job at quantifying this point.

- Acquiring a new customer can cost five times more than retaining an existing customer.
- Increasing customer retention by 5% can increase profits from 25-95%.
- The success rate of selling to a customer you already have is 60-70%, while the success rate of selling to a new customer is 5-20%.

So often in sales, we "move on" after we have sold a client. What if we spend time and energy staying connected and adding value to current and potential Avatar customers? Your sales cost would go down, your time and energy management would improve, and your profitability would improve. Your past satisfied clients have the most Trust in you! Do you have a list of your current and/or past customers that you stay connected with? What is the next step with each to stay connected and add value?

This is where Sales and Production and/or Operations need to stay connected. Many Software as a Service companies (SAAS) have these departments separate and bifurcated. To keep satisfied customers, these departments need to work together to ensure success. I recommend that all companies track and review a customer retention metric. If you want to scale, you can't keep losing customers.

Mike Stover was a thoughtful, intelligent leader who wanted to win and lead in the right way. He was a terrific and loyal company leader and was part of a senior team that worked with us previously. We identified him as a potential Avatar customer. We stayed in contact every time we came into town. He went to our annual conferences to learn and network. Two years later, Mike got a chance to lead in a new district and saw there was a business need that we could solve. He called us and we carried out a very successful implementation in his region under his leadership. Mike is a good friend to this day and we stay in contact. I cherish the confidence he had in our team.

Susan Sharp first worked with us in London. We developed a great relationship and delivered on a difficult to measure ROI project. We stayed connected to her throughout the years as she was the type of Avatar customer we worked well for. She was passionate about leadership and improvement. She cared for her people and her company and believed in good process. She attended several "Best of the Best" events. I think she loved being around like-minded leaders and got energy for her own efforts to help drive change as a leader. We visited her several times to share what we were learning. When she landed a VP job in California and later in Salt Lake City, she trusted that we could help her deliver on her change mandate. We delivered on our promises and helped the plants she was involved in to improve. How much is two-way trust worth?

Always stay connected. Always add value to your past Avatar customers.

What your customer wants most of all from you is somebody to trust. When you help them win, you will win. There are many ways to earn trust as we have discussed in this chapter. Keep thinking of their needs and thinking of their win. That will motivate and inspire you to do things that will build trust.

The Hang-out Test

Be the type of person your client would want to hang out with. We used to have a recruiting standard when we hired new project managers. Does he/she pass the "hang-out" test? We used to take them to lunch or dinner after the interview and see how interesting or interested they were. Some recruits talked too much and some talked too little and some didn't engage.

Think about this concept as far as being a trusted advisor. Are you interesting enough to hang out with? Do you ask great questions and show interest in them? Do you have diverse and interesting hobbies and topics to speak on? Do you talk too much? Do you talk too little? Would you be interesting to a new client?

This is one of the longest chapters in the book. It is that way for a reason, because if you can learn how to become a trusted advisor, you are well on your way to making it Rain. I hope you will review each one of the principles taught in this chapter and apply it to your situation.

Application Questions:
1. What have you done well to become a trusted partner?
2. What could you do better to become a trusted partner?
3. What can you do to better prepare with specific insights for your potential customer?
4. What are your best open-ended questions to learn your potential customers' pain points?
5. What are creative ways to keep connected to your warm leads that haven't gone to *done deal*?
6. What current or past customers should you be staying connected to?

Chapter 5

Trust the Sales Process

Tanner wanted to make the President's Club in his new company. The top 10 out of 70 account reps would win the award, the associated trip, and the recognition. Tanner did win the award and recounts how he won:

"The #1 factor that got me there is 'my process'. What I mean by that is, for example, during the summer months, I wasn't seeing too many deals come through. Most reps would get discouraged and wait for a big deal to close to then make them motivated to work harder. Instead, I determined that if I focused on my process, I could succeed even when my numbers weren't succeeding. I knew that if I stacked highly productive days on top of each other, those were wins. At the end of the day, the results came. It's all about judging your process and not your results."

Define a Process that Works

Most salespeople know the sales system from their point of view. Most sales systems look something like this:

- Prospecting
- Presentation/meeting
- Handling objections
- Closing
- Follow-up

I found it more powerful to look at the sales process from the clients' outcomes. How do they view the sales process? I used a three-point sales system:

Awareness

Demonstrating Value & Trust

Aligning the Close

1. Awareness

This isn't a marketing book that is going to teach you in detail on how to fill the top of your funnel. I will mention a few of my favorites and then spend more time teaching principles and show examples how to move through the sales process with trust.

Your potential client needs to become aware of you. Here are the major ways to generate leads:

- Various types of cold calls (internal or external groups)
- Industry conferences or tradeshows
- Advertising (print, billboard, online, TV, radio, podcast, etc.)
- Referrals from past satisfied customers

This is the top of sales funnel. How can you get your Avatar client to become aware enough to accept a meeting with you or buy your product? All of the methods to bring potential customers to the top of your sales funnel work better with trust.

The best lead generation method for you will work best with two principles: Targeted and Warm Introductions.

A. Targeted Introductions

Facebook and Google have made billions of dollars by offering companies targeted introductions. Their algorithms show your products and services to those who have bought or shown interest in similar products. That's why they collect the information they do ... so they can most effectively and efficiently use your lead generation dollars. The same principles hold true for professional service firms. General 'lead generation' dollars and time isn't as effective as targeted methods. If you sell to senior leaders, you need to be where they are at. I have found some industry associations and forums are tremendous ways to meet your Avatar customers, but make sure and do your homework. Spend the time and money on advertising and conferences where your ideal customer is at. If your Avatar customer attends a certain conference, go to that conference. If your Avatar customer reads a certain magazine, then advertise in that magazine. Don't waste lead generation dollars by throwing advertising at everybody.

    B. Warm Introductions

Warm Introductions get you in the door and build trust faster!

Whatever lead generation you use, make sure it's targeted and as warm as possible. I personally don't like cold calling. I do like warm calling. If you can get an introduction to a potential client by somebody they trust, then you have increased your possibilities significantly of advancing the deal. That is why in advertising, the introductions are done by potential people you trust in the public eye. We admire certain athletes and they can warm up an introduction to a certain product or service. Testimonials are also used in advertising to warm up the likelihood of advancing in the sales process. My local window washing, lawn service, tree service, and pest control all try to accelerate the lead generation process by telling me my neighbors use their service and they would be happy to tell me how good their service is.

In professional services, a warm introduction is critical. If a trusted peer introduces your firm, you will advance in the sales process. I would say 100% of the deals in our business as we 100x our company were "warmed" at various points in the sales process.

My Two Favorite Lead Generation Ideas

My two best "targeted" and "warm" introduction methods for lead generation are past client referrals and industry conferences.

Client Referrals

This is a very underutilized method.

Some people feel uncomfortable with asking past clients for referrals. "I can't impose on them." "That is too bold." "What if I upset them?" I would respond two-fold: Do you really believe your product or service will make the potential client better? Did you deliver an extreme amount of value and deliver on your promises? If you can answer yes to both, then do it.

As a young consultant, I spent a lot of time with two clients, Darrell and Greg. We built solid relationships outside of work on the golf course and squash court. Most importantly, we delivered on our promises and made their life and career better. I trusted them and they trusted me. They were then happy to introduce me and my company to their sister companies and some competitors. I am extremely grateful for their confidence in me and our services.

James Bowzer and I had a lot of fun improving the performance of his region. When he was promoted to head office, he went out of his way to introduce us to his boss and peers. We ended up working with many of them. Why? Jim trusted that we wouldn't make him look bad. He trusted us that we could help his company. He was putting his reputation on the line by introducing us.

I will never forget the trust that Jim, Bill, Kevin, Helene, Bill, Peter, Greg, Gary, Larry, Larry, Gary, Sue, Steve, Doug, Mike, Scott, Dan, and many others gave us to both work with them and introduce us to their peers. You only have so many referrals. You will need other warm lead generation ideas to meet your budgets.

Industry Conferences or Trade Shows

My second favorite lead generation method is targeted industry conferences. Not all conferences are the same and not all lead generation methods at the conference are equal.

Remember to only go to the industry conferences where your ideal customer will be.

While at the conference, don't fall into just standing at the booth waiting for them to come to you. **Be Proactive** and have a plan.

<u>Develop Warm Introductions Before you go to the Conference</u>

The most effective ways to get warm introductions:
1. Target which Avatar customers are attending the event.
2. Reach out and set up meetings before the event.
3. Use Peer introductions via email or social media. Search LinkedIn and find out who is connected to who. If a past customer knows your potential Avatar customer, then ask for an introduction. Many times, if they know them well enough, they are willing, and this is a very effective way to get a meeting.
4. Research the company's background and potential needs of your Avatar customer attendees.

If you have an Executive Advisory Council (EAC), bring them to the conferences. An EAC member is usually a retired trusted leader who advises and supports your company (I will talk about the EAC more specifically in the chapter on Continuous Improvement and Innovation). I remember walking a Shanghai Industry conference with Gary Yesavage and Ate Visser from our EAC. They were both retired executives from large and reputable companies. I thought I was walking with Rockstars. They knew everybody. We met with people that we didn't even know were attending the conference. We set up good meetings with many Avatar customers. Trust and Trustworthiness sells!

Never Turn Off Your Lead Generation System

This is a particular problem for Professional Services. We get so busy with "working" the deal or providing value for the client that lead generation is constantly in "Start and Stop" mode. It tends to be the last thing that gets attention. I like the way that SAAS companies have done their sales. They have a full-time dedicated lead generation team so the funnel never goes dry.

Solution: Build in permanent steps to have lead generation going continuously. Hire an employee(s) who is accountable for it or contract it out. I would say the biggest fault of professional sales firms is that they don't have a fluid and continuous process for lead generation. Most firms do well at closing deals. They just don't have enough qualified 'avatar customer' leads coming in the top of the funnel.

Make your **Awareness** (lead generation) process warm, targeted, and continuous, and you will have permanent RAIN.

Never Leave a Meeting without a Natural Next Step

This is a very important principle in progressing deals. You should always be thinking before, during, or after the meeting, how do I progress this opportunity? What is the natural next step that is in the client's best interest?

If you have listened well for pain points and then articulated well how your service meets the potential customer's pain points, the next step can be easy and natural. Always share during your presentation some ideas on potential next steps. Also, make sure you leave 10 minutes at the end of the meeting for a discussion on next steps. Some salespeople get so excited about their product that they run the presentation right to the end of the meeting and then hope for a quick agreement. That is not a best practice.

My favorite way to move to next steps is to ask the potential client what they think should be the next step. This open-ended question allows discussion to happen and also allows the next step to come from the client's mouth. It is their idea what to do next. I may suggest other ideas through my question set to get to an ideal outcome. If they suggest a next meeting with their boss or key decision makers, then I may ask, who should be involved? When do you want to have it? What additional information do you need to see to make the best decision for your company?

Don't get too excited that they agreed to a meeting and then seek to close the meeting too soon. This is a perfect time to gather more intelligence and needs to close the deal. This is why I always leave plenty of time at the end of the meeting for discussion and intel gathering. Don't miss this opportunity. Sometimes they need to have a discussion among themselves. It is a best-case scenario when they have time and are comfortable to have that discussion on the call/meeting with you. You can help facilitate the discussion and listen for each parties' potential agreements and objections.

This information is golden. Too many salespeople talk too much. Too many salespeople don't effectively manage the time of the meeting. Your best tool to advance a deal is your question set – your question set to get the meeting going and your question set to discuss next steps. Create an environment for open discussion at the beginning, middle, and the end of the meeting.

The worst first meeting is a meeting where the salesperson talks most of the time and asks for the deal at the end.

Other Potential Next Steps

Sometimes you don't get an ideal next step. Sometimes the potential customer doesn't understand the value yet. Keep the discussion going and probe and search for potential next steps.

Here is the continuum of potential next steps (from strongest to weakest):
    a. They ask for a contract
    b. They ask for a proposal (more on this later)
    c. They suggest a next meeting date
    d. They ask for references
    e. They ask for more information
    f. They suggest they will get back to you after a discussion
    g. No thanks. It's not for us.

Worst case scenario, you can promise to be in touch. You can ask if it's okay to follow-up with them in four weeks. You can ask them if they would be open to getting occasional information from you on potential needs they have expressed.

Of course, we would love to go to contract and deal after every meeting, but that probably doesn't happen every time. You may need to be very intentional on keeping them "top of mind" to send them value-added information and to "warm-up" the deal.

Can you move to contract or proposal too quickly?

Yes! I am always leery when selling "big ticket" promises and services of moving too quickly to proposal and contract. Take your time to get proper stakeholder alignment and to properly understand their needs. If you rush to proposal and write a generic proposal, it most often will fail during closing and stakeholder alignment. The "big boss" may veto the generic proposal because you haven't taken the time to truly understand the needs and for the potential client to really understand your value versus the cost. That is why referencing is so key. Ideally, you want your potential customer to reference before the price discussion.

In SAAS sales, you can also move to "done deal" too quickly. You must deal with the potential issues upfront. You can clarify issues without scaring them off. I have seen too many account reps get the deal signed, only for it to fall apart a month after the process is implemented. "My sales rep didn't tell me this was going to happen." "They didn't tell me you needed this type of information from us." Surprises after the deal is done never goes well. The goal is to get a happy and satisfied long-term client. Never get a deal done for your quota and not think long-term. If you want to be a RainMaker, you have to think about this on every done deal:

How can I make sure this client remains a long-term client and a great reference or referral?

We need this client to be a great long-term reference in order to be a RainMaker. Bad work or bad service travels fast. It will catch up with you. You need the implementation to go fantastic to 100x your company. Be fanatical about the success of your client after the deal is done.

Here is the ideal process if you're going to get a win-win deal:
1. First meeting with agreement for a next meeting.
2. Second meeting with all the decision makers. Prepared agenda to have discussion of needs and solutions.
3. Referencing of your past clients. A well-planned agenda with "results one-pagers" of your work. More on this in the next section.
4. Request for Proposal with details from the client on the results needed.
5. Co-write your proposal with lead client delegate.

6. Co-present your proposal with the lead client delegate to the entire decision-making team.
7. Signed Contract.
8. Provide excellent service and or product.
9. Referrals and References to support your future lead generation.

I realize that the ideal doesn't happen all the time, but it is helpful to clearly understand what a win-win process looks like.

The following sections will teach the principles on how to demonstrate your value properly and align the stakeholder for a win-win deal.

2. Demonstrating Value and Trust

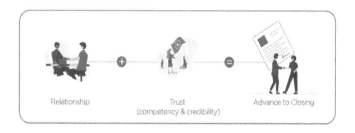

Relationship Trust (competency & credibility) Advance to Closing

Turning Leads into Customers

Once you get a lead, how do you build enough trust to advance to closing? The key next step after your initial meeting is to demonstrate the value of your product or service. If you're in SAAS sales, you will need to demonstrate your actual product. In professional services, you will need to demonstrate your service. While you are demonstrating your product, your real goal is to advance the relationship, show competency, and build credibility for you and your firm. Many salespeople get confused at this stage; they assume it's just about your "spiel". Some salespeople think meeting success is if they finished their presentation. Wrong! Your real objectives are three-fold: 1. Build a rapport. 2. Show your competency for their need. 3. Illustrate your credibility to deliver on your promises. The meetings change dramatically when you're clear on these outcomes.

In the online world, these outcomes can happen quickly. Seth Nielson[4] helps course creators grow their brand, impact, and income. He sent me an email one day. I (like you) get hundreds of unwanted emails a day. Seth's was different. It was apparent that he had researched my site and knew something about my book and my courses. He had mentioned how much he liked some of them and also shared an idea on how I can improve sales. He shared a link to set up a free exploratory call. We had one short call together and I bought his yearly program.

Why did I say yes to Seth even though most marketing emails go unanswered? He did his homework. He understood my business. He was kind and considerate and he knew his material. I had a business need and he clearly described how his services could help my business. We went from awareness, relationship, credibility, competency, and alignment very quickly.

Some sales aren't that quick. Our sales cycle in consulting could take up to one year. Most of that time was spent in relationship and trust building.

Relationship Building

Every sales book written since the beginning of time has included this variable in it. Think about it. Have you ever bought anything from any salesperson that you didn't like? Usually not (or not for long). The key characteristics I see in sales relationships are:

a. Showing interest in others
b. Genuine care and concern

My mother-in-law and wife are great relationship builders. They love to ask questions to find out how you are doing. They do homework ahead of time on social media (or other means) to see what is going on in your life. If your favorite sport is basketball, they start to follow and love basketball so they can show interest in what you care about. Sales relationship building is the same way.

People don't want to know how much you know until they know how much you care.

My mother and father taught me that all the time. It is a simple principle but so true. We want to associate with people that show genuine care and concern for our well-being. Even in the competitive business world. It still comes down to how much you care about others. If you come off as an arrogant know-it-all, sales are not for you.

"Whatever interests my client interests the Heck out of me."

This was one of our favorite sayings while growing our company. We said it with a tongue-in-cheek laugh, but there is truth to it. I never knew I would have this much knowledge and interest about Nebraska NCAA football, but one of my favorite clients was into it so I became interested. You might think that this is manipulative, but if it's done with genuine interest to build a relationship and help out a client, it works!

Remember, we care so much about our cause and we care so much for our clients that we will do any ethical means necessary to help them.

Bob was one of our best salespeople and consultants. His clients called him affectionately "Coach Bob". Bob was a "client interest first" type of person. You often had a conversation with Bob and after 30 minutes, you have told your whole life story and he has hardly said a word. All he did was ask very client-centered 'interest' type questions. Bob was also a magic man with positive recognition. Even with the first meeting, Bob would go out of his way to find specific and meaningful things the company and the individual was doing. After a meeting with Bob, you were willing to buy almost anything. Bob genuinely showed interest and cared.

Part of Deon's success (mentioned in Chapter 2) was also through building relationships of trust based on empathy and understanding. Deon sold his company for hundreds of millions. He had 1,200 sales reps. I asked him which sales reps were the best and why. He said unequivocally, "The ones that can build genuine relationships the fastest. A key to building relationships was to listen and genuinely empathize with the client's problems and pain."

As you are building a relationship, it is also important to be building competence and credibility (Trust). One of the best ways is to have your past customers sell for you. If you can get your future clients to talk to your past clients, you can accelerate your deals.

Accelerating Trust in the Process

Referencing is an under-utilized step in the Sales cycle.

Many people are wary of salespeople because we have earned a reputation of not having their best interest in mind. The quickest way to overcome that concern is to have your potential customer talk to or interact with past customers. In other words, have them interact with peers or people that they trust who have had a good experience with your product or service. The online industry does this all the time by having athletes or influencers talk about their experience with your product. If we trust that influencer, we generally buy that product if we perceive the need.

Three Ways to Reference Future Clients to Past Clients

1. Referral Calls or Meetings

After the first meeting, if they were interested in our service, we asked them to reference our past client. We made the reference process as easy as possible. We set up the call. We gave each party background materials. In particular, we crafted a one-page success story with the past client. The one-page always had the return on investment (ROI) achieved by working with us. We knew if we could make referencing easy and get them to talk to past customers, we could increase the trust significantly and move quickly to alignment and close.

2. Client Conference

Client conferences can be a very powerful tool to convert interested potential clients into paying clients and Trusted business partners. At our annual meeting and "Best of the Best" ceremony and dinner, we recognized the top projects and results of the year. The project manager that was responsible and the clients stood up and gave a short speech while they received their trophy and "black jackets". It was a twist on the "green jackets" awarded to Masters golf tournament winners. If we could get potential clients to attend, we almost always worked with them.

The conference was well planned out for months. We didn't leave anything for chance. We knew if we could get an interested client to attend, we could close business. We would carefully pick the "expert speakers" and past client speakers to highlight value to our client and reinforce the power of our work. One year the theme was safety performance improvement, and another year the theme was "step change" in performance. The speakers were asked to share the results, learnings, victories, and areas for improvement. Many clients attended just for the learnings and perspectives from other change agents in various industries.

One of my favorite stories (this type of thing happened fairly often) was when a Senior VP of a large multi-national company stood up and said, "RLG partnering with our leadership team helped with a $1B turnaround in performance during an 18-month period." Sitting here were 50 VPs in the audience that could hire us and they just heard a peer talk about the scale and magnitude of our work. The trust and credibility for our company went sky high.

We worked hard to get our clients and potential clients at this annual event. We knew if we could get potential clients to attend, we could accelerate our trust, credibility, and sales. We had a senior management team of 12 people who would make personal invites for executives to attend nine months before the event. About once a month, we would review the list on our weekly call and determine attendees and potential attendees.

Another year, a Senior VP stood up and said that our company helped turnaround their company and prepare it for sale. The division was rewarded with a $500 million increase in sales because of the work we had done together.

Create environments where trust, competency, and credibility can be clearly seen and you will 100x your company.

3. Executive Advisory Council

The third method we used to accelerate trust was to develop our own Executive Advisory Council (EAC), which I mentioned earlier in this book. The role of the council is to advise us on our strategy and also to introduce us to peers who may have potential problems that we could help. We asked them to provide referrals to relevant potential customers. EAC members were retired and trusted leaders of their industries. Gary Yesavage was our most successful EAC member. Gary had worked with us in his role as President of Manufacturing before he retired. We had built a good relationship and delivered on our promises for bottom-line results. When he retired, we asked him to join our EAC. He was fantastic in introducing us to his peers who were our Avatar customer. Why? Gary had trust with his peers. Gary was a trustworthy person. It made all the difference in the world to our business. Trust sells!

3. Aligning the Close

There are many factors that go into closing the deal, but the two most important are "handling objections" and "aligning the decision makers". This is where many salespeople lose the deal. They grow impatient and lack understanding about what is happening from a client's point of view. They don't understand all the complexities and alignment that needs to go into selling a large deal.

Be prepared and expect to deal with objections such as price and be prepared to help with alignment.

<u>Alignment in Decision-making</u>

Very rarely will one person make the decision for the deal. Even if they are the CEO, they will want to get buy-in and alignment among their team. This process takes patience and deep insight on how to help get alignment to close the deal. The best method to align is to ask early and often: "Who else will need to buy-in for this deal to go through?" Some people overestimate their own ability to close the deal inside of their own organization. Always determine ways to get other decision makers in on the sales calls and reference calls.

Rob Gulbronson and I got a reference from a past satisfied customer. The referral went to the VP of supply chain. He insisted he wanted to "vet" us out first before recommending us to senior management. We were able to impress him enough that he wanted to go to referencing.

We highly encouraged him to have other decision makers on the referencing calls. We insisted that it would make his job easier. He invited three other people to the three referencing calls. One was the VP of operations who was the ultimate decision maker. We started work two months later and we are still working with that client some five years later. It began with a good pitch meeting, but what really sold them was talking to our clients. We made sure that all the decisions makers were on those calls so we could get to alignment, and close easier and faster.

You might ask, why would your clients go out of their way to speak so passionately for you? The answer is simple. If you have extraordinary customer care, build incredible relationships of trust, deliver for them, and make them look good, they will be your best advocate.

Handling Objections

"Everybody has a plan until they get punched in the mouth."
~Mike Tyson

Sales is easy when it all goes to plan, but the RainMakers know there will be objections and know how to handle them with great customer care.

A. *Always Clarify the Concern*

The first step in handling any objections is to clarify the reason for the question. Don't panic; don't freeze up. Calmly ask an open-end clarifying question about why this is a problem or concern.

A successful sales engineer from a SAAS company recently told me this story. "A year ago, we lost a large client because we didn't have an ADP integration. This year, the client came back to us and asked if we had the integration complete." They hadn't completed it. He said this time, the account executive asked, "Why is an ADP integration so important to you?" The client went on to tell him why. The sales engineer was able to say that they could do the integration through a different method and solved the problem even more effectively. The contract was signed within the week.

Deon, who was introduced earlier in Chapter 2, had a relevant and significant experience on handling objections while he was trying to scale his credit repair business. He sat down with the VP of a large bank and was hoping to sign them up as an online marketing affiliate. The VP came into their first meeting with a cross to bear. He unloaded on Deon and his team. He accused them of getting people's credit repaired that didn't deserve it. The VP said, "They had made mistakes and didn't pay people back and don't deserve to get relief." The VP was mad. Have you ever been in a meeting like that? It's hard not to lose your cool or at least get rattled. Deon had the presence to be able to calmly ask the VP clarifying questions on why he felt that way. The open-ended questions by Deon helped the VP talk and air out his concerns. He felt listened to. Then, when Deon felt like the VP was ready to listen, he talked about several things that helped him see the issue from the other side. "Many people don't know how the credit system works," Deon said. He also highlighted that Deon's company's sweet spot was the people with a 650 credit score and he helped them get to 750. It turns out, the 650 to 750 credit score people were the "Avatar Customer" for the bank. He also explained their affiliate marketing program and the financial benefits to the bank. Deon walked away from that encounter with a large affiliate for his company.

How you deal with an upset or angry potential client:
    1. Don't overreact. Remain calm.
    2. Remember your purpose and cause.
    3. Ask open-ended questions to understand.

4. Articulate your value and benefit to the customer.

Sometimes the biggest objectors make the best clients.

B. Price Objections

RainMakers don't give up margin.

I have never worked or coached anybody that has the lowest cost product or service. I have always been on the side of higher price and higher value.

I believe if you're going to work with a client, you must give 120% and you deserve a fair margin in return.

I strongly believe that companies that deliver on their promises deserve to earn a good return on their products or services.

For example, Apple has been able to earn high returns because their products are exceptional. Tesla has terrific margins because their product is one of a kind. If you follow the process in this book, you will be able to charge more for your products and services.

Your client may say something like: "I like what you're talking about, but you are too expensive. I can hire three engineers for the price of your service." You can respond with an open-ended question to clarify the exact concern. It will be obvious to you by his comment already that he is just looking at this as a cost problem. You want to turn the discussion into a Value discussion. Or in our case, a return-on-investment discussion. To overcome their concerns on cost, I would usually show them stories about a four-to-one return on investment in 12 months on their costs. I would then translate that into how many more dollars into their factory. If they didn't acknowledge this benefit, I would usually ask, "Would you be willing to talk to your peer in XYZ company about the ROI they got on their investment? They had the same concern that you do about hiring more employees versus investing in performance improvement capability for the whole team."

Five Solutions for Clarified Price Objections

1. Not an Avatar customer
2. Emphasize Value over Cost
3. Risk/Reward Contracts
4. Build more Trust
5. Free Offer

Let's look at each of the categories listed above in more detail.

1. Not an Avatar customer

Not all deals will get done, even if you are a RainMaker.

There are some companies that don't think win-win. They only believe in win-lose. I don't want to sell to those type of organizations.
Fortunately, these types of companies are the exception. Probably the most extreme example of this was with a major multi-national company that was the darling of their industry. Their growth and profitability were the envy of the entire industry. When we went into our first meeting, we were unequivocally told that we were way overpriced and that they were already doing the type of performance improvement we had talked about. They called our work "basic" and "simple". We never went back to that company. It was clear we were selling at the right level (senior management), but they simply didn't have the characteristics of our Avatar customer. Interestingly, they were in the news five years later. The company collapsed under the weight of a huge accounting scandal. They went from darling to villain fast.

I have mentioned this earlier, but it would be important to underline the importance of clearly identifying your Avatar customer characteristics. Our Avatar customer needed a certain level of honesty and openness to perceive the need for help and support. If they didn't have a level of proper "self-awareness", we weren't going to be successful in selling this customer.

It is best to "know when to walk away" as the old Kenny Roger's Gambler song said. Sometimes the best and most cost-effective solution is to "fold" and focus on other potential Avatar customers.

I know this is hard to do. We are all competitive and want to win every deal. But the truth is that if you want to 100x your company, you can't focus too long on customers that don't fit your Avatar needs and characteristics. We all have limited time and energy. Focus on the 25 Avatar customers who have the right characteristics. You won't be sorry.

2. Emphasize Value Over Cost

It's an investment, not a cost.

This is another very valuable tool in your closing tool kit. Most clients will have price concerns. Anticipate it! What are the top three objections you usually get? Prepare for them and seed them into the early conversations. Price concerns always came up in selling non-tangible promises, such as consulting services. Early and often in the discussion, we would emphasize return-on-investment (ROI). It's a lazy way to sell when you go to discount without thoroughly covering the benefit over cost. In the first discussion and right through to referencing, I would emphasize ROI in every discussion. Save your clients from their obsessive focus on only cost versus value. I had a president of a company call me upset that his plant managers couldn't see the ROI, they only saw the cost. It's a sad commentary that some corporate cultures are held more to their costs versus overall benefit.

Another strategy to help them see the investment point of view was to use their own data. We would find out what a 1% improvement would equate to for their division. We would then do the math to illustrate if we improved costs in their division by 5%, that would equate to $50M in savings, and our services would cost them $5M. That's a 10-to-1 return on their money in 12-18 months.

In addition, we added, you will have an engaged workforce, better leadership, and a sustainable process for the plant once we are gone. Do you think this ROI and these benefits are worth the investment? If they had the need and we had built some trust, this type of discussion helped overcome the price concerns most of the time.

Salespeople, don't be lazy on this one! It's too easy to give discounts. Prepare in advance for the price objection. Do your homework and find 'like' success stories that illustrate benefits over cost. Break down those benefits into tangible and non-tangible. Many decision makers want to see and understand both types of benefits for their company.

3. Risk/Reward Contracts

Once in a while, a client would ask us to do a risk/reward contract. Meaning, we would reduce our fees and take a percentage of the benefit. If it was a trustworthy Avatar customer who we had confidence would partner well, we did a risk/reward deal and it worked well for both parties 90% of time. So well that our clients stopped asking for this option. If you trust the leader and are confident in your product, this is a very attractive strategy to get into a new industry. Make sure you have a 'crystal clear' contract on how to execute the contract. Trust and verify through good contracts.

4. Build more Trust

If I have built a significant relationship of trust, then it can overcome any price concerns.

If my customer is so confident I can deliver on my promises, then price won't be a stumbling block to getting a deal done.

If there are still concerns, go back to the drawing board with your team. Is this a potential Avatar customer with the right characteristics?

What can we do to build more trust? Go back to referencing? Go back over ROI? Invite them to our annual meeting?

Go back to some of the 'value added' ideas mentioned above to see if you can close the deal.

5. Free Offer

If the customer still isn't convinced of your value despite following the process that I have outlined above, then there is another way to build trust while protecting your right to earn margin. Offer a 'Free Limited Time' test or pilot of your product or service. For example, if you are an online coach, then offer a free 20-minute introductory coaching session to try and establish trust for full-time work. If you are a consultancy, offer a free (with expenses) one-week assessment of their department or operation. This allows your team to come in and build trust by adding value. Show your client that you "mean them no harm". This is such an important principle in selling professional services. People assume the process will be painful, time-consuming, and perhaps more so, embarrassing.

If you can go in and start the assessment process with the clients for one week and show them your approach and style, you will build tremendous trust. We didn't make this offer all the time, but if we knew the client was very interested but still had price or trust concerns, this 'free' approach closed the deals 95% of the time. This should be used selectively and only with interested "ideal clients".

Online businesses offer free 7 days trials all the time. Why? Because it works. You start using the software and realize that it is easy to use and will provide value, then you buy the whole service.

What if they still want a price deal?

Sometimes you can nail this process and stress "value over price" at the beginning, middle, and end and the client still wants a deal. They want to feel special. There is a psychological component to price negotiations. Everybody wants a good deal.

If your client is still needing a deal, then give non-monetary benefits. You have been listening during all the meetings and discussions on what the client values. There are a number of non-monetary benefits you can offer that may feel like a deal for them.

Some ideas:
- Give them 3 extra days of my time (senior executive) to support the project.
- Our head office training can have 10 training seats instead of just 5.

- We can do the work one month faster and save you one month of billing.

There are a number of ways you can maintain your margins and help the client feel special and like they are getting a deal.

Systematize and Automate the Sales Process

Nick Pass is extremely successful at door-to-door sales. He has worked very hard and doesn't get discouraged by a "no". He has always believed in the process. After so many no's, he will get a yes. It's just numbers.

After being super successful and earning incomes that most 20-somethings only dream of, he got a chance to recruit and manage a large team of door-to-door salespeople. Nick and his partner Ty Fox have worked just as hard in systematizing and automating the sales process so his team of 200 can also be successful. He has automated the business development process (BD) that we will discuss in the next chapter. Each phase of the BD process has a measure versus a target. The lead generation team can see and be accountable for their numbers as can the closing and installation teams.

He has systematized the lead generation process from internal and external lead sources so that the closers already have verified leads. The closers are jumping to his team because of the systems he has put in place to help every phase of the sales process to be successful.

If you want to scale your business, it can't be just personality lead. If it is, it falls apart when the leader leaves. You have to understand your sales process and systematize and automate every phase so it operates like clockwork. It works even when you're not.

Pro tip: Make sure your Customer Relationship Manager (CRM) has questions to capture all the decision makers and influencers in your sales database. This will help you understand the decision-making process and proactively include them in the sales process. If you don't include them, you rely on your client lead articulating your benefits and value proposition for you. Generally, they will not do as good a job as you will.

Also, add this question to your CRM, "Did I ask them for a referral?" If you are a trusted partner and have delivered extreme value, they will have no problem sharing your story.

Here is a summary table for this chapter. It highlights the best practices in the 3 phases of the Client sales:

Sales Process
How do we fill the process with Trust?

LEADS	DEMONSTRATIONS	CLOSING
Best Practices:	Best Practices:	Best Practices:
▸ Consistent	▸ Preparation	▸ Referencing
▸ Warm leads	▸ Listening for Pain points	▸ Multiple Decision Makers
▸ Targeted (Avatar)	▸ Articulating to Pain points	▸ Value based selling
	▸ Value/Outcome	▸ Handling Price objections
	▸ Next Steps	

Application Questions:
1. How are you going to get more leads with your Avatar customer?
2. What can you do to build trust faster during the sales process?
3. Who are the decision makers on the deal you are working on right now? How can you increase your influence with the key decision makers?
4. How can you improve how you deal with Price Objections?
5. How could you further systematize and automate your sales process?

Chapter 6

The Business Development System

This is the engine that drives the sales process. You can't just have any engine; you must have the right engine based on your Avatar customer. If your business development system is set up for just any customer, it will track the wrong activities.

Most companies are using Customer Relationship Management (CRM) systems today. I love them because they can automate your key performance indicators and make them visible. Here is the catch: many of the CRMs aren't measuring the right metrics. They are too generic. They are not measuring activities to the Avatar customer and they don't track the sales process from the customer's points of view.

If you can modify your CRM to track the right metrics for your customer, then you have a good process that will drive more sales.

The Truth about being a RainMaker

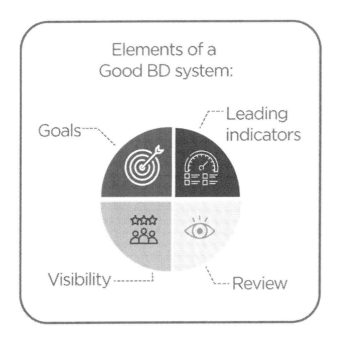

If you have all four parts of the BD system working consistently and it is measuring to your Avatar customer, you just won the sales lottery. The whole BD system is captured in this quote:

"When we deal in Generalities, we rarely succeed.
When we deal in specifics, we rarely fail.
When performance is measured, performance improves.
When performance is measured and reported, the rate of improvement accelerates."

~Thomas S. Monson

Goals

Most companies have sales targets and or budgets. Make sure you have those sales budgets set for each team and each individual. You need granularity and specificity for these budgets to be motivating.

It is important to set the right level of targets and budgets for your sales teams. The Goldilocks principle applies here. The targets can't be too low or too high, but have to be "just right". It is worth the time to get these budgets just right.

In my experience, the most motivating targets have the following principles:
1. Improvement over last year.
2. Will help the company meet their overall goals.
3. Not so aggressive that it's unmotivating for your sales team.

Most companies just work on levels. If you meet that level, then you are bonused. I also like to reinforce growth over last year. If my sales team has improved 25% over last year but didn't meet their quota, that should be rewarded.

Lay out the targets very clearly and don't change them for a year. Super motivated sales representatives will figure out how to hit your targets if they are done properly. This is a win-win for everybody.

Leading Indicator

This point is essential if your BD system is going to drive the right behaviors and the right results. You must identify the right leading indicator that drives the results you desire.

The lagging results are your sales, but what are the predicting activities that drive those sales? Measure and focus on those activities and you will have a system that drives performance. I recommend 80% of the focus on the leading indicators that drive the results you desire. For example, if the number of cold calls determines your success, then measure that as your Key Leading Indicator. Many sales organizations know that they close 10% of all cold calls they make. The key is then to increase the number of calls you make. Cold calls aren't painless and it can be easy to get discouraged and demotivated. Make sure and track the number of calls and make performance visible. This will keep your team accountable and motivated to keep this activity moving.

In my consulting business, the key measure was the number of senior leaders I had calls or meaningful interaction with. If I could increase that number, I was going to increase sales. In our CRM, we tracked the number of senior manager quality interactions.

A successful real estate client has a goal to sell 50 homes per year. Lead generation is a key leading indicator for success. She has her lead generation metric broken down to track: # of open houses, # of past client referrals, # of agent referrals, and # of online leads. She focuses on meeting the leading indicator targets to deliver on her goal of selling 50 homes. She knows the conversion rate from each lead generation source. For example, past client referrals have a higher conversion percentage than online leads.

Another real estate leading indicator example: Open houses convert 10% of leads from every open house. If she needs 10 sales from open houses this year and she usually gets 10 leads per open house, she needs 10 open houses to accomplish her goal of 10 sales (exact numbers not shared for confidentiality reasons). At that point, it's a math formula. She sets up a spreadsheet to figure out how many leads she needs by type to sell 50 homes. She knows exactly what she needs to do to sell 50 homes. It's a process! Develop and trust the process!

Every industry has their own set of leading indicators. The key is finding the right ones.

Let me give you a non-sales example to bring the point home of the importance of finding and tracking the right leading indicators. I once worked with a VP of Operations named Bill. His team had a very good safety program, but they worked in a very hazardous environment. Bill wanted to change the behaviors and the results of this health, safety, and environment (HSE) program. This is a very difficult area to measure and improve. Accidents and incidents can happen in so many ways when you have hundreds of employees working in hazardous areas. Bill and his senior team identified two leading indicators that eventually led his team to zero incidents. Yes, *Zero* safety and environmental accidents for one year. This was unheard of in his company and his industry.

They did many actions to improve the performance, but the engine was the two leading indicators that drove great plans, behaviors, and actions. He tracked the number of positive interventions by his senior team and number of safety catches by front-line employees. He measured and reviewed each one in the appropriate team meetings. For instance, on Friday morning, he and his senior team presented a graph with each team leaders' name on it showing how many safety leadership interventions happened that week. It could have been attending a safety meeting or giving an "atta boy" to an employee, etc.

Each week, each team member saw their contribution to the target as compared to their peers. Why did this work so dramatically? They had specifics, they had accountability, visibility, and review. It all started with identifying the right leading indicator of success. Bill's assumption was that his leadership team could change the culture and the performance one positive interaction at a time. He was right!

Examples of Sales Leading Indicators:
- # of Cold calls
- # of Warm calls
- # of Meetings with your Avatar client
- # of BD hours
- # of Leads

Visibility and Review

My pet peeve is New Year's resolutions that are set and then so quickly forgotten and given up on. If this resolution is important to you, make it visible and reviewed. Here is the best way I have seen companies make performance visible:
- On a whiteboard in the team office
- On a PowerPoint presentation shared and reviewed once per week
- In a newsletter
- In a graph on a bulletin board
- On everybody's computer or phone each morning

Every company has a desire to be a culture of positive accountability. Accountability is such a buzzword today, but very few know how to create a system where positive accountability is fostered. Here is the secret: have specific goals, make them visible, and make sure they are reviewed on a regular basis. Many companies skip the review. They assume that people are paying attention to the boards or the reports. They get 20% of the value of their BD system by not creating opportunities for 'bottom-up' accountability meetings. You must have monthly bottom-up accountability meetings to review sales leading and lagging indicators.

When we first went in to work with the largest airplane manufacturer in the world, they did have a monthly goal review meeting. The VP and the CFO stood at the front of the room and reviewed the metrics for two hours. We changed the meeting to have leading indicators and had the front-line manager report their own efforts (not the CFO). That is what I mean by bottom-up – the person responsible for the activity and the result reported on the performance. That is real accountability. People will prepare and develop change all month to make sure they look and perform well next month in front of their peers.

By the way, this meeting was reduced to 60 minutes following these principles and their performance improved.

Positive Accountability and Support

What if you are stuck in a sales rut? What if you know the right BD activities to do, but still are not making it happen?

Robin was a top insurance salesperson. He then contracted Covid-19 and had long lasting Covid effects. Food didn't taste good, smells bothered him, and he had migraine headaches regularly. He felt horrible most of the time. This went on for 18 months. His life and work started to suffer. He felt bad for not being able to do what he did so naturally in the past. Discouragement and depression set in. Fortunately, Robin believed in continuous improvement and positive accountability to kickstart himself.

Robin knew that business prospecting was a key activity for future sales. He couldn't bring himself to do it. He started sending me his "prospecting" result from last week and his plans for next week. Just a little positive accountability got Robin moving again despite his lack of energy. The encouragement and accountability from a trusted advisor got him back on track.

How to Make Your CRM Work for You

One of the fastest growing sectors in business is the automated CRM. As mentioned previously, I love this idea and the concept of automating your BD system, but there are two main causes for failure:

1. They measure the wrong leading indicators.
2. They aren't used in a Sales Review.

I know several companies where sales representatives track their own metrics because the CRM doesn't track the proper process and metrics. I also know many companies who have a good system, but it is not used to review performance.

What do you do if your sales people don't like process?

In one of my recent Sales Training events, Dawson made this comment: "I have run a successful financial planning business for 15 years and done well with relationship building, working hard, and knowing what products are best for what people. I see now that if I really want to scale this business, I need to have a process and follow the process."

Some salespeople just like building relationships and working hard and don't enjoy the rigor and discipline of a Sales Process. The key to overcoming this tendency is by having great CRM sales reviews that drive accountability, collaboration, and get results.

1. Every Account Rep tracks their own one-pager from your CRM.
2. The one-pagers have the following sections: name, date, lagging metric vs. goal, leading metric(s) vs. goal, and action plans to improve for next month. The action plans should be in a "who does what by when" format. The bottom section of a one-pager should be "Highlights" and "Recognition". This last section helps to share best practices and build positive teamwork.
3. The Account Rep has to share his one-pager with his team once a month.

Keep the review simple, positive, and specific. Each rep should only go 10 minutes. Part of the experience is to see if your reps can share their data in a crisp and appropriate fashion.

This sales review, if done properly, will drive your reps to work their hearts out to look good for next month's review. Many times, companies just rely on 1-1 leader follow-up with a salesperson or they rely on the incentive system to drive the right behaviors and results. I am suggesting building a simple but dynamic monthly sales meeting that drives focus, accountability, engagement, and positive recognition to drive bottom-line sales.

Tom Leavitt runs a very successful machinery business headquartered out of Langley, British Columbia, Canada. He bought this business from a large multi-national company that didn't view it as strategic. Tom has grown the company revenues and EBITDA (earnings before interest, taxes, depreciation, and amortization) 700% since buying it over 20 years ago. Tom, Brian (CFO, his brother), and the senior team understand accountability. For many years, they have run this performance management system that I have been describing. I sat in a sales meeting recently where the team reviewed their metrics on a whiteboard in the middle of the office every Friday. Each sales rep reviewed his key leading indicators versus plan and talked about one action they were working on to improve. The whole meeting was 30 minutes. Incidentally, the team had increased sales over 200% that year.

In consulting, we had a very powerful quarterly business review where each one of our Business Unit leaders had to present their lagging and leading key performance indicators to BATT (Baseline, Actual, Target, and Trend). It showed a clear picture of whether you were ahead of the previous year and the target or behind. This type of accountability was precise and accurate. I've seen too many accountability meetings where people can stand up and fake their way through a presentation. With a good business review, you will feel super empowered and super accountable for the numbers and the subsequent action plans. You will work all quarter on the results and the presentation. That is accountability! The system created the accountability. The process holds us accountable for performance.

When performance is measured, performance improves. When performance is measured and reported, performance accelerates!

Application Exercises:
1. What are the lagging results/goals that you want to achieve?
2. What are the leading indicators that will help you achieve those goals?
3. How can you make performance visible?
4. When will you review performance publicly?

Chapter 7

Continuous Improvement and Innovation

"Early Success can be the death of long-term success."
~Rick Heyland

Many times, organizations and people get stuck because they have had success in the past. "This is the way we did it 5 years ago to be successful, therefore, this is the way we will do it now" or "Let's not stray from the formula that brought us success". This argument is compelling but wrong. The environment is changing so fast. The economy is changing so fast. Public opinion changes so fast. Technology changes so fast. Industry priorities change. Your Avatar customer may change. Your Avatar customer needs may change.

If you are not innovating, you will stop growing!

A 100x person and organization is programmed for change. They are programmed with what Carol Dweck calls a growth mindset in her book, "Mindset - The New Psychology of Success." A RainMaker is energized by learning.

They always are seeking to get better. They love to learn from everything. Every time they win a deal, they learn from it. Every time they lose a deal, they learn from it.

A simple way to learn is to ask three why's. Here is an example: Why did we win the deal? Because the client had a business need. Why did the client acknowledge a business need? Because they opened up and shared with us. Why did they share with us? Because we asked good, safe open-ended questions and because we made them feel comfortable at the beginning of the call. You can see that you can keep asking why until all the learnings are out. Don't stop at three why's if the learnings are still coming out.

If you truly are open to learning and continuous improvement, you will influence your entire organization. Your curious, open, and growth mindset will influence all of your department and other departments in the company. So many learnings will come out and result in improvements ... in your product, your packaging, your sales deck, etc. Remember to be patient when influencing other departments. Be a positive change agent.

When we first opened up the safety improvement part of our offer with Gary Christman in Alaska, it demanded that all our departments take action to change our offer and our materials. Take the initiative and help others move into continuous improvement. Some of your best sales work will happen in your own company.

    Always Be Innovating (ABI). Many times in sales, your products are on a life cycle. Either the competition has copied your product or a new and improved product has replaced it. It is the same in consulting. We found that the margins for our upstream energy client were reducing and the competition had gotten fierce. We wanted to expand our work in manufacturing, but had very fewer connections and stories. So, we did something that medium-sized companies don't usually do. We started an Executive Advisory Council with past satisfied clients from manufacturing. These leaders gave us many 'warm' introductions and our manufacturing business started to outpace our upstream business. At a time when our competitors were stagnant, we were on another growth curve to help us accomplish the 100x gains.

    Brett Heyland is the president of a giftware company. He owns this business with his brothers-in-law. They sell candle warmer and home fragrance products to large and medium-sized giftware retailers. Think Walmart, Target, Hobby Lobby, and more regional retail chains. They have grown company revenue 10x what it was when they bought the company in 2008. They've learned valuable lessons on identifying their "ideal customer" and doing everything to service them well. One of the key success factors in their growth story is that they are always product-innovating to meet the changing needs and priorities of their customers. In 2016, they jumped outside their existing product categories and added essential oils, diffusers, and other aromatherapy products to their line for the first time. Their sales doubled within 18 months. They've also innovated with new distribution channels. After years of selling mostly to brick and mortar retailers, they built a robust e-commerce business. When COVID hit and their brick & mortar stores closed down, e-commerce kept their business afloat. Had they not innovated over the years, their sales may have stagnated or decreased.

Innovation sells!

Personal Continuous Improvement

This principle also applies to your skill set as a salesperson. Always be learning and improving on your skills. Read, listen, and go to conferences that will help you improve your selling, trust, and relationship skills. You will be better 10 years from now and more successful in sales if you continually improve. Please don't have a fixed mindset and determine that you are not good at 'closing' or 'relationships' or 'small talk'. Learn from the best and ask for advice from people who are better at a skill than you are. Always be curious. This will keep you in a learning mindset. Ask more senior people out to lunch and ask for advice. Ask your boss for feedback that will help your skills improve. Sign up for courses that can help your skill set, mindset, and tool set to be a RainMaker. Set a leading indicator to learn. How many books will you read to improve? How many training courses will you go to? How many 'advice' lunches will you set up? How many podcasts will you listen to?

What skills should I work on?

I believe the top three skills to be a RainMaker are:

What about relationship building, asking good questions, listening, trust building, closing, and presenting? Yes, they are very important. The three outlined above will drive all the other skills you need. If you are clear on your motivation (purpose), you will be relentless in support of growing and learning all the skills. If you are always curious learning from others, you will learn the other skills. Besides, people like being around curious people. They ask good questions and have meaningful conversations. If you have good personal organizational skills, you will find the time to do all the things you need to do to be a RainMaker!

<u>Delegation is also a Key Skill</u>

You might be a bit overwhelmed by the list above. Remember, you don't have to be great at everything. You can delegate or partner with others in your organization to bring all the necessary skill sets to be a RainMaker. If you aren't as good at numbers, make sure you have a Rob Gulbronson on the team. Rob was an engineer and he could bring an ROI to a client to the decimal point in any presentation. I had many executive assistants over the years that kept me organized. Queenie Tsang would schedule a meeting to review my progress on my top 25 Avatar customers and review my next steps. It takes a team to become a RainMaker.

Where does your motivation come from to always be learning and improving? Your why, your cause, and your purpose!

Application Exercices :
1. Ask three Why's on the last deal you won. What did you learn?
2. Ask three Why's on the last deal you lost. What did you learn?
3. What Avatar customers' needs are changing?
4. What skills do you need to improve on?

Chapter 8

Be Your Best Every Day

How are you going to find the energy and determination to do all that I have outlined in this sales system?

A key part of high energy and determination comes from your purpose. You are selling a noble cause that all "ideal customers" will benefit greatly from. Another key source of motivation and energy comes from excellent self-care. If I am going to be the best for my clients, I need to practice great habits of self-care. It isn't just something people with lots of time do. It's the habits that Top RainMakers prioritize in their routines. To be the top RainMaker in your industry, you need to have great habits in the morning. You can't afford to bring low energy to any meeting or call. Start each day with what my friend, Todd Sylvester[5], calls the "hour of power". From one hour of self-care, you can generate the energy, enthusiasm, and determination to be your best every day.

I recommend in that hour you do something to build physical, spiritual, and emotional capability. To illustrate, with 30 minutes of exercise, 10 minutes of deep breathing work, and 20 minutes of inspiration/spiritual reading and writing, you can build reserves to help you accomplish your goals and overcome the setbacks that each day can present.

Todd Sylvester has been sober for over 30 years. He has an incredible story of rescue from a life of drug and alcohol abuse. Today he is a mindset coach and counselor. He is also a very successful podcaster, speaker, author, and inspiration to thousands. He has a top 1% podcast called, "Todd inspires Beliefcast" and over one million people have listened to his stories. They have found hope and strength in his words and those of his guests. He is also a successful husband and father. How does he do it all? Todd credits his hour of power. He arises early in the morning and accomplishes at least three things before anybody wakes up: prayer, exercise, and reading inspiration material such as James Allen's book, "James Allen Classics Collection." It gives him the energy and capability to be a top RainMaker in his field of work!

The following is a list of attributed practices that can help you be your best every day.

Gratitude

Gratitude is also a key practice of a RainMaker. I included a lengthy gratitude section in my book, "Live Your Purpose - A Step by Step Guide on How to Live Your Best Life." I highlighted studies that show over 10 benefits of having healthy gratitude in your life. They include better health, more stamina, and improved happiness among the list. I personally have been writing morning gratitude journaling for the last 15 years. I wish I would have started in my twenties. Our brains naturally want to focus on the gaps, the opportunities, and the problems. A regular gratitude practice helps you start each day focusing on the wins. It helps you focus on the positives. It helps you be a better and more positive parent, spouse, leader, and influencer. How would you like to hang out with a person that just focuses on the problems, who doesn't recognize what is going right? Start your day out proper by focusing on the blessing and the wins. It will make a huge difference in how you work with people and clients throughout the day.

Do you want to fasttrack your relationship and trust building? Be grateful for your clients, staff, and peers. For example, If you are intentionally grateful for your clients, it will radiate in your countenance and attitude with them. Be grateful for their time. Be grateful for them sharing with you their problems and strengths. Be grateful they gave you a follow-up meeting. When you are grateful for your clients, then you show up as caring, respectful, and positive instead of a "pest" just trying to work the process for a big sale. Try it. Gratitude pays, even in sales.

Physical Capacity

Charles Duhigg in his book, "Power of Habit", calls exercise the keystone habit that leads to many other positive habits in your life.

The Mayo Clinic cites seven benefits to regular exercise: (Mayo Clinic website-October 8, 2021)[6]
1. Exercise controls weight
2. Exercise combats health conditions and disease
3. Exercise improves mood
4. Exercise boosts energy
5. Exercise promotes better sleep
6. Exercise puts the spark back in your sex life
7. Exercise can be fun and social

Because of all those benefits, you will be a better RainMaker. You will outlast those who don't regularly exercise. My experience over my 35-year career is that regular exercise (6 days a week for 30 minutes) will make you more sales and more money.

Sleep and Eating Right

If you want to be a high performer over a long period of time, you have to eat and sleep right. I know these are motherhood statements you have been told all your life. I know when you're young you can get away with abusing these two principles and make it through college or your first few years at work, but it won't sustain. If you want to be a successful RainMaker for a sustained period of time, you need at least 7 hours of sleep and to eat right. Eating right means not eating late. Reduce your sugar and eat more plant-based food. There is so much research coming out that shows the mental, physical, and emotional benefit of eating more plant-based.

Michael Greger, MD the founder of Nurtritionfacts.org, wrote a great book titled, "How Not to Die." He shared research study after study showing how eating right can prevent and reverse disease. He says, "It turns out a more plant-based diet may help prevent, treat, and reverse every single one of our 15 leading causes of death." The top 15 causes of death include heart disease, cancers, brain disease, diabetes, kidney disease, suicide, and Parkinson's disease. Be disciplined in how you eat and you will be able to be a RainMaker for a long time!

Clients respect salespeople who practice what they preach. Who takes care of their bodies and minds? It used to be a badge of honor if you worked many hours per week. We thought people would respect us. In sales, you only have a few minutes to make a first and lasting impression. You can't handle objections or questions effectively if you haven't had the right amount of sleep or proper energy by eating right. Maybe other careers that are less 'client centered' can get away with not taking care of your sleeping and eating, but in sales, it is critical that you are at your best each client-facing moment.

The latest research shows that you can be more effective at work if you get the required amount of sleep. You have better health, better mood control, and handle stress better.

All the latest research shows a high correlation between eating right and cognitive decision making. Your ability to handle objections from your potential client may well depend on what you eat and how much sleep you've been getting. If you want to be great at sales over a long time, you need to take care of your body.

I have a coaching client who works 80-90 hours a week and carries that work ethic around like a medal. His peers recognize him because he is always working. His clients even recognize how hard he works, but there is a shadow side. He has increasingly noticed how stressed he is and has admitted he's not as sharp in some key meetings. I believe less work and more sleep will increase his sales effectiveness significantly.

Emotional Capacity

I didn't learn to take care of my emotional self until I was well into my forties. I found myself earning millions of dollars, having a full and happy family life, and still often felt stressed and anxious. I read the "Power of Now" by Eckhart Tolle and it changed my perspective. I learned that I needed to take better care of my emotional self in order to be the best I can be. I started to do breath work and mediation. I found that I was sleeping better and was less anxious after 10 minutes of meditation. In the rainmaking business, you can become very future focused and anxious for the next big deal. Eckhart Tolle taught me that the other side of the coin for emotional happiness is to focus on the now. If you let your mind go uncontrolled, it will start to focus on the future and rob your happiness in the now. "If only, if I can land this big deal, then I will relax or go on vacation." If you find yourself saying something like this, you would benefit greatly by learning to slow yourself down by being happy in the present. The concept is called mindfulness. It's a terrific concept that I wish I had learned and developed capacity and skill for in my twenties. I hope that you will add this skill to become a better RainMaker, provider, and person.

I read an interesting book by Susan David, PHD called "Emotional Agility" that supports the benefit of emotional capacity. She quotes some research that says, "Magazine salesmen who mindfully sell more subscriptions ... It's the quality of being fully present and available that audiences relate most to". She defines mindfulness as, "Paying attention on purpose and without judgment". Can you see how this skill can help you be a top RainMaker?

How to Deal with Stress and Setbacks

Many of my coaching sessions with high performance people involve how to properly deal with the stress and setbacks that occur from having big goals and ambitions.

<u>Rubber Band Analogy</u>

Imagine your effectiveness is represented by a rubber band. If the rubber band is slack, you're not working hard and not hitting your personal and professional goals. If the rubber band is too tight, it's under stress and it's about to break. Peak performance is found with tension on the rubber band, but not too much. Having good self-care practices builds elasticity for your emotional, physical, and spiritual self. It allows you to maximize your performance over a long time.

Now that we have addressed ways to proactively deal with stress with exercise, gratitude, and meditation, what do you do to deal with emotional upsets when they occur?

Dealing with Upsets: Getting Unstuck

Despite building in stress capability with good self-care habits, some setbacks can take your breath away and set you off emotionally.

How do you deal with losing a big sale? How do you deal with an upsetting email from your boss? How do you deal with upset kids? How do you deal with an argument with your spouse? These are important topics that all of us cope with in the pursuit to greatness. How do you reset from an upsetting experience? Here are some ideas that have worked for the high performers I have dealt with:

- Sleep it off. Wake up refreshed to start anew.
- Breathing work. 10 deep breaths to reset your energy.
- Take a walk.
- Don't respond right away. E.g., if you get an upsetting email, wait 30-60 minutes to respond.
- Exercise.
- Read inspiring literature.
- Focus on what is going well. Write it down.
- Talk it out with a trusted partner.

Perspective

If I had one gift for everybody that struggles with stress and emotional setback, it would be the skill to find the right long-term perspective. "This too shall pass" is a wonderful perspective. Sometimes when you lose a big deal, it is hard to find the right perspective.

I remember being on a flight and getting an email that a client wanted to cancel a large sale and program we had just started. I was devastated. It felt like a gut punch. This would have a significant impact on our budget for the year. It would mean not hitting our growth targets for the year. I had done my exercise and hour of power in the morning before the flight, but this one really hit the panic button inside.

Losing this new sale would be a huge setback for me and my team.

I started to spiral a bit and panic inside. I reached for inspirational literature that had comforted me before. I was reading about a story of war and thought to myself, how is this going to help me with my current panic? As I continued to read, I found the words that brought a huge comfort to me. It said the people in the war story were able "to find peace to our souls" through great "faith" and they found "hope". These words helped me find perspective. By the end of the flight, I felt a calm inside. I found the perspective to properly deal with the problem. I was able to think rightly on how to deal with the problem. I 'ran to the problem' and was able to gain the trust of the key check signer to continue the program despite the financial troubles they were in as a company. If I wouldn't have been able to calm down and find the right 'client centric' focus, I wouldn't have been able to help the client see this was best for his company.

We did go on to significantly help the company's financial troubles and formed a strong long-term partnership with the company and the leadership team.

Live your Best LIFE PLANNER

I am passionate about helping people with the 'how'. Most of us know the things we should be doing, but struggle sometimes to practice the habits that will help us be successful. For this reason, I have developed a planner and sell it on Amazon (Live Your Best Life Planner) to help people plan this type of self-care and self-

sustainability habits in their lives. The planner includes a section for the following:
- Purpose Statement
- Goals
- Action Plans
- Daily Gratitude and Learnings
- Daily Prioritized Planning

I developed it so you can build the practices and habits in place to be the top RainMaker in your industry. I have on my website a free pdf of my "Live your Best Life Planner" if you want to start using it to crush your sales goals.

Build your capacity and capability every day through great routines and habits. Willpower can be fleeting but habits, procedures, and routines are lasting. By building these routines, you will be able to be successful in your sales career and respond appropriately to setbacks that occur. These habits will also help you to become a more well-rounded person and excel at the other important roles in your life. Don't be so busy that you don't take the time to make yourself better for the long run!

Sustainability

We don't want you to be the best RainMaker for one year and then burnout. I have seen many people do this. They had all the skills, all the charisma, but none of the self-sustainability practices. The stress burned them out in a year or two. With good self-care habits, you can be great for 20 or 30 years!

Application Exercise:
1. What could you do to improve your self-care in the morning so you can be your best every day?
2. How will you measure your progress to your commitments from question 1?

Chapter 9

Conclusion

Myself and many of the sales leaders I highlighted in this book have 100x their companies. I believe you can do the same. It will take more than just hard work. You will need to work smart. You will need to apply these 7 steps and build a sales system that works and is sustainable over time.

As we discussed at the beginning of the book, a RainMaker is a person who attempts to cause rain to fall, either by rituals or by a scientific technique.

Following these 7 rituals and proven processes I have shown, you will Make it Rain!

Trust the Process

A very famous quote in sports is to "Trust the process." Nick Saban, Bill Bellicheck (New England Patriots), and the Philadelphia 76ers (NBA) all quote this mantra.

Nick Saban, as we talked about in Chapter 1, is arguably the most successful NCAA coach by any measure. Read the following quotes by him about having and trusting the process:

"Know what you want to accomplish and focus on the process rather than the outcome."

"Success will continue only as long as the commitment to the process of being successful remains in place."

"Everybody wants to be a success. Not everybody is willing to do what they have to do to achieve it."

Are you ready to be disciplined? Are you ready to commit to the process?

Take the free 5-minute RainMaker assessment on Ci4life.org to determine where you are in your journey to be a True RainMaker.

You can also go to my website: Ci4life.org to get Freebies and Tools to help you on your journey.

Good luck! If you need coaching help and support, email me at rheyland@gmail.com.

About the Author

Rick Heyland retired as COO Americas of RLG International in 2018. He is now the President of Continuous Improvement 4 Life (CI4life). Ci4life is dedicated to helping organizations and individuals live their best life. Rick is also the author of the bestselling book, "Live Your Purpose - A Step by Step Guide on How to Live Your Best Life." Go to www.ci4life.org for details about Rick and his products and services.

Rick lives in Draper, Utah with his wife, Cheryl. They have six children and 15 grandchildren.

Acknowledgments

I am eternally grateful for the blessing of being married to my kind and generous wife, Cheryl. What a blessing to be on this journey with her and our 6 kids and 15 grandkids.

I am also very grateful for my colleagues at RLG International who together accomplished some terrific growth of our business together. These stories are equally their victories and accomplishments. I will probably miss some names but in honor of acknowledgment, I would specifically like to thank the following colleagues at RLG: Rick Mazur, Keith Cross, Ken Fawcett, David Helewka, Jerry Weisendfelder, Roger Laing, Taylor Davis, Rob Gulbronson, Chris Payne, Mike Morgan, Queenie Tsang, John Shewfeldt, Bill Nash, James Parnell (since passed away but always beloved), Peter Boersma, and Don Telfer. You all have made a tremendous difference to my career and my life.

To our Clients who made all of this possible, without your Trust and partnership, these learnings and results would have never been possible.

To Marianne Thompson for being my terrific editor on both my books and Andy Highland for doing a great job on graphics and the book cover. Thanks for being such great partners.

References

Books

Emotional Agility *by Susan David, PhD*

How Not to Die *by Michael Greger, MD*

James Allen Classics Collection *by James Allen*

Live Your Best Life Planner *by Rick Heyland*

Live Your Purpose - A Step by Step Guide on How to Live Your Best Life *by Rick Heyland*

Mindset: The New Psychology of Success *by Carol Dweck*

Power of Habit *by Charles Duhigg*

Power of Now *by Eckhart Tolle*

Trust-based Selling *by Charles H. Green*

The Trusted Advisor *by Charles H. Green*

The Trusted Advisor Field Book *by Charles H. Green*

Podcasts

Pat Flynn – The Smart Passive Income podcast

Rick Heyland – Continuous Improvement 4 Life

Dr. Ani Rostomyan – The Nutrigenomics Pharmacist

Todd Sylvester – Belief podcast, @Tsinspires

Websites

1. Harvard.edu. Corporate Purpose and Financial Performance. (https://dash.harvard.edu/bitstream/handle/1/30903237/17-023.pdf)

2. Ci4life.org

3. Ci4life.org Millennial Money course. (https://ci4life.org/millennial-money/)

4. Seth Nielsen: staula.com

5. Todd Sylvester: toddsylvester.com

6. Mayo Clinic.com

Rick Heyland is a world-leading performance coach who previously authored anAmazon bestseller: "Live Your Purpose: A Step by Step Guide on How to Live Your Best Life". As a management consultant for 32 years, Rick has real world experience on how to grow and scale companies.

Rick retired in 2018 as COO Americas from RLG International. Today, he runs a performance improvement coaching company called CI4life (Continuous Improvement 4 Life).